"Outstanding book. Describes the various conflict styles and uses animals and chess pieces to reflect each style. I highly recommend this book for its easy-to-read style, its applicability to the workplace, for interpersonal relationships, and for life in general".

—Dr. Pat Farmer, Organization Consultant & Personality Analyst

# SOCIAL CHESS

# SOCIAL
# CHESS

## What Role Do You Occupy
## In Your Relationships?

Dr. Christopher Beverly

iUniverse, Inc.
New York  Lincoln  Shanghai

Social Chess
What Role Do You Occupy In Your Relationships?

iUniverse books may be ordered through booksellers or by contacting:

iUniverse
2021 Pine Lake Road, Suite 100
Lincoln, NE 68512
www.iuniverse.com
1-800-Authors (1-800-288-4677)

ISBN: 978-0-595-43004-8 (pbk)
ISBN: 978-0-595-87345-6 (ebk)

Printed in the United States of America

# Contents

# Acknowledgements

Without the support and contributions of several individuals, I couldn't have written this book.

A special thank you to:

*Mary Lou Beverly,* for teaching me to always trust my heart. Without your unconditional support and love, I never would have pursued a graduate degree in psychology, gone to California in the first place, or had the confidence to become what I am today. I love you.

*Brett Thomas Beverly,* for teaching me to stand up to authority when it's not being reasonable—and you know who I'm talking about—and yes, for finding the document on Mom's computer when I thought it was lost, you Social Wolf, you. Love you, man.

*Jim Jones—The Art Man,* for putting some kick-ass illustrations in this book. Great job!

# So You're a People-Watcher?

Me too!

I confess.

Watching people is fun.

It's not that we mean to watch people—it's just so darned fun, right?

If you love watching people, and I suspect that you do, this book can help you better understand yourself and your closest relationships.

# What is Social Chess?

Social Chess is a new approach used to study group behavior and relationships from a personal point of view.

Let me give you an example.

A group is like a chessboard. And five pieces exist on this "group chessboard".

Every situation that involves people who know each other well will resemble this chessboard—and therefore these five pieces must be considered.

All of the pieces are equal in Social Chess. In the *game of Chess*, the pieces are ascribed different values—in *Social Chess*, each piece is merely different.

The first piece, the often-debating *Social Wolf*, wants to be right most of the time, and prefers to win.

The second piece, the helpful *Social Lynx*, prefers to attend to the entire group, and often tactfully avoids conflict.

The third piece, the harmonious *Social Panda*, doesn't want to be in conflict in the first place, and only conflicts with others when forced to do so.

The fourth piece, the fun loving *Social Kangaroo*, prefers to conflict with others just enough to keep things "interesting", often by entertaining and will win quickly if the opportunity presents itself.

The fifth piece, the strong willed *Social Badger*, enters into conflict because of its character, and only backs down when shown respect by the other party.

These five styles describe niches people occupy in their close relationships—which are best understood as a group chessboard.

The author of this book is a Social Lynx, who prefers to make "points" (constantly he is told), but is less concerned with winning and losing once his point has been made! He also has a unique social drive and his social interactions and lifestyle resembles one of the pieces in chess—but you'll have to read further to learn more about his style.

This book reveals the conflict style you occupy in your closest relationships and seven laws that govern all group interactions. Read on!

# Preface

Completing a dissertation on conflict and personality left me wanting something more. My dissertation involved studying conflict using empirical methods, and the process of completing such a thorough project taught me the value of investigating a subject from a detached, scientific perspective. Because my dissertation involved administering questionnaires in a controlled setting, the results could be used to advance conflict theory in my field, organization development, and this fact was intrinsically satisfying to a certain degree.

What I learned from completing a dissertation, earning a doctorate in the social sciences, and writing Social Chess, is that I derive more satisfaction from presenting information to public audiences than academic audiences. I do, of course, highly value the theory development process, and have learned the value of the scientific perspective. The public, caring less about advancing academic theory and more about applying information to their personal lives, motivated me to reflect on my life experiences and write *Social Chess*.

# How to Read This Book

To enjoy this book, you must enjoy studying people. *Really* enjoy studying people.

If you have a Ph.D. in psychometrics or experimental psychology and have picked up this book to analyze its methodology, skip to the end of the book and read the "Note to Academics" section first.

If you are curious about people and want to learn more about how they relate in group settings from a personalized perspective, you'll enjoy this book.

There are many different ways to approach reading this book. Here are a few suggestions:

*You could:*

Read it from cover to cover. This would allow you to get the most out of the book.

Just read "What is this book about?", "Development of the Theory", "Is Social Chess Similar to Chess", "Pieces on the Board: A Model", "Distinguishing Types", and "The Seven Laws of Social Dynamics" if you're in a hurry.

Just skim it and read the captions in the illustrations to get the gist of the book.

# Who is this book for?

This book is for anyone who loves to learn about how people act in groups and in their relationships. If you want to enhance your understanding of people you know well, this is the book for you. Anyone with an open mind who is willing to study social situations and relationships in *new and creative ways* will benefit from the information reviewed in this book. For those with advanced social science backgrounds who appreciate applied studies that incorporate qualitative methodologies, this book is also highly recommended.

# Development of the Theory

I strongly believe that during group interactions with people who know us well, our personalities *change*. Each of us has a *group personality*. Some might say that only our behavior changes when we're immersed in our social circles—but I would argue that we have a "collective personality", one that we have when we are with certain people—or at least people we're around often.

Have you ever realized you get really serious or really silly around certain people? That certain people draw *out* a certain side of you?

Groups have parts—everyone contributes in certain ways—and people play roles for the group to function. Not only do people have to play roles in order for the group to function, but people often occupy a niche in a group.

But do people always occupy a niche?

People are more likely to do the same things over and over again if they know others in the group well. Then they are much more likely to play a role, or occupy a niche in a group.

But what keeps a person in that group niche? *Conflict.*

People's preferences for how they deal with conflict reveal the niche they prefer to occupy in a well established group, and I call this niche their *conflict style*. It's what comes most naturally to them when they're socializing with those they know well.

Social Chess Theory is the notion that relationships are best understood in a *group context*, and that once people know one another well, they occupy natural roles in their relationships.

# How I became interested in Group Dynamics

Learning about people and how they relate to others has always been one of my passions. Understanding what motivates people, how they make decisions, and why they behave and think the way they do is the primary reason I pursued graduate study in the social sciences. Since I was very young, I had a knack for influencing groups, especially large, formal ones—for example, I starred as the Prince of Pollution in an elementary school play and was often the superstar if a situation involved serving or teaching people. It also became apparent to me—and hurt me—that everyone didn't share my enthusiasm for influencing the collective mindset.

People love talking about themselves. Most know this, and many people dread hearing about other people's lives for hours on end. One-way conversations can be hard to bear at times—especially if the other party takes no interest in what you have to say. I learned from an early age that people really enjoyed talking about themselves and that it can be fun to listen (a lot of the time—not all of the time). I have always talked a lot myself—but I also can be a patient listener when the situation calls for it. Focusing on the other person more than myself has taught me a great deal about human nature.

Every group has its own "collective personality". This collective, or group personality, consists of individual personalities, of course. And although every individual contributes to the group, not every individual makes the same contribution to the group dynamic. For example, my mother has always been a very gentle woman (and still is). Usually laid back, my mother was and is rarely confrontational; conflict does not suit her style. My father, who is no longer with us, was usually direct and competitive; his style more outcome-oriented than confrontational, he often got his way, especially with me. On the other hand, I have always applied a mix of assertiveness and kindness to social relations, but usually lean toward assertiveness.

The combination of my mother's and father's personalities, along with my own, yielded an interesting group dynamic during my adolescent years. My kind and assertive "sides" were often on display as a teenager, but I discovered that any alteration in my behavior changed the group dynamic—sometimes drastically. My mother was influenced more by behavior that threatened to de-harmonize the group dynamic, whereas my father paid more attention to anything that distracted from activities or tasks. Every group dynamic is different, and when people know one another well, one of them can easily change a dynamic—and this person doesn't have to be the most powerful or mature person in the group. This was especially true in my case, because I would often destabilize the dynamic without realizing why I was doing so.

Group dynamics change moment-by-moment and can alter drastically over time. This is why ignoring a group member who doesn't appear to be playing an important role is done at your peril, because this individual can become the centerpiece of a social interaction in the future. One person may be the star of the show, but another person often rises to challenge their stature. A third person, previously ignored and not considered important may suddenly take a major role by mediating between the two starring competitors. And although the mediator is more motivated by peace than fame, he nonetheless appreciates being recognized for his efforts. It serves us well to remember that historical greatness always involves groups—never just one person acting alone—and groups can reposition in a moment, forever changing events.

You can change who you are. Your behavior is malleable. That is, you can become anyone you want, and do anything you want if you put your mind to it. It is also true that if you've always been a jokester, you can decide to be serious for a time. Roles are flexible—especially if everyone in the group is different. In a diverse group, there is no overarching norm, no rigid boundaries defining what is acceptable and not acceptable.

It can and probably will be difficult to change who you are. Behaviors can be difficult to change, and you will encounter formidable challenges. If you're a jokester most of the time, people will not understand why you are suddenly being so serious—people typecast each other for simplicity's sake. If you're in an environment where everyone acts similarly, you'll encounter a mindset, a groupthink that will attempt to impose boundaries that will test your willingness to be unique.

Be unique anyway.

People will eventually get over the fact you've changed—often they will admire you for it after the fact.

My life experiences and formal education in the social sciences inspired me to embark on a journey. This journey took me to the east and west coasts of the United States, and taught me more than I could have ever learned within the confines of a classroom. These insights have helped me create a book that can serve as a tool for anyone who enjoys social interaction, social science, and enhancing their understanding of people and relationships. I hope you enjoy reading this book as much I enjoyed creating it.

# Is Social Chess similar to Chess?

*Not really!* Because Social Chess is a theoretical model used to explain the mechanisms and parts of groups, similarities between Social Chess and Chess the game are more *metaphorical than real*. Those looking for dissimilarities between Social Chess and the game of Chess will have much to discuss.

This is not a book about Chess—this is a book that uses the Chessboard and its five pieces as a metaphor to examine the nature of group behavior. The five "pieces on the "board" (*discussed later*) do not possess different values in Social Chess; they merely reflect different styles of socializing and relating to others in groups.

Comments that suggest the book does not capture the true essence of Chess will be ignored—because the book does *not* capture the true essence of Chess.

This is not Chess—this is Social Chess, a way of examining relationships and group behavior from the inside.

# The "Pieces on the Board"
# Which Social Chess Conflict Style
# fits you?

The next several sections will be used to help you determine which Conflict Style fits you.

*What is your "natural" conflict style?*

Your *natural conflict style* is the style you employ when you aren't trying—it's the style that comes most naturally to you in your closest relationships, *once those closest to you know the real you.*

There are five conflict styles. You employ all five of these conflict styles in your interpersonal relationships—with family, with friends, and with coworkers.

One of these styles comes most naturally in your closest relationships, however, and in this next section you want to find out which style *fits you best—not which style fits you perfectly—because none of these profiles perfectly describes your natural conflict style.*

For this next section, think about how you behave in your closest relationships. Who are you closest to? Your parents? Your brother? Sister? Husband? Friends? Your Boss? A Coworker?

Think about two people you're very close to.

# The Five Conflict Styles

There are five distinct conflict "styles".

These five conflict styles are:

1. The Social Wolf

2. The Social Lynx

3. The Social Panda

4. The Social Kangaroo

5. The Social Badger

As you will see later, we are all part Social Wolf, Social Lynx, Social Panda, Social Kangaroo, and Social Badger—but we tend to express characteristics similar to one of these social "animals" in our close relationships more often than the other four—and this is our "natural" conflict style.

A few tips as you go through these profiles:

a. **You should see parts of yourself in all five profiles, but one style comes most naturally to you in your closest relationships.** Because you employ all five styles in your relationships, you are likely to exhibit characteristics similar to those reviewed in all five of the profiles—you are not, however, likely to have more than one natural conflict style in your closest relationships.

b. **You probably have a reputation for being a certain way in your family or within your social circle—there is a reason for this.** What you perceive your conflict style to be is more accurate than what others perceive it to be—however, remember to keep in mind how people who know you well perceive you and what they have told you about their relationship with you. This can help you decide which conflict style most closely resembles your natural style.

c. **Be honest.** Seeing ourselves objectively can be difficult, especially since who we are in our closest relationships defines us. Remember that each type has its own role in every social circle.

d. **Use the hybrid styles to assist your judgment.** The hybrid styles are included to clarify your assessment and help you decide which profile best fits you—you'll find these hybrids are combinations of animals, and reflect who you resemble when the environment requires that you act in a certain way. This is who you have to be, not who you would like to be or who you naturally are.

e. **Read the "distinguishing types" section that reviews some of the differences and similarities between the Social Chess Conflict Styles.** The differences and similarities between the five styles differentiate the subtleties that distinguish one type from another. You should find this section particularly useful.

# Social Chess: Pieces on the Board—A Model

| Conflict Style | Social Drive | Willingness to ENTER conflict | Conditions for ENDING conflict |
|---|---|---|---|
| Wolf | Activity-driven | High—they don't perceive debating as "conflict" | Prefers to win/be right |
| Kangaroo | Process-driven | Moderate—prefers things stay "interesting" but becomes uncomfortable with too much conflict | Prefers to win, but-compromises quickly |
| Panda | Peace-driven | Low—Strongly dislikes conflict and is very flexible in order to avoid conflict | Doesn't see conflict in terms of "winners" and "losers" |
| Lynx | Group-driven | Low—Doesn't like conflict and uses tact and humor to defuse tension | Prefers to make a "point", less concerned about how much they "win" |
| Badger | Truth-driven | Moderate—Who they are draws them into conflict with others, but they don't seek conflict | Prefers to win, must get respect |

# Social Wolf

## THE SOCIAL WOLF (NOUN)

*A SOCIAL CREATURE THAT PREFERS FAMILIAR SOCIAL ENVIRONMENTS, ENJOYS DEBATING ABOUT TOPICS SHE/HE KNOWS WELL, AND PREFERS TO "WIN" BY EXHIBITING EXPERTISE ON A GIVEN TOPIC.*

*Conflict Style:* Wolf

*Social Drive: Activity-driven:* the lifestyle of Wolves is often defined by activities they enjoy (and yes, other things as well).

*What draws a Social Wolf info conflict with other people?* Anything. Wolves love to "spar"—a good, lively debate is usually welcomed by Wolves, who are always *looking* for new ways to win a debate about something they're passionate about.

*When will a Social Wolf want to get out of conflict with another person?* When they're convinced they've won, they're ahead on points, or they're just tired of arguing for the sake of it with someone who won't debate according to the established "rules".

**Wolf-Friendly Environments:** *Familiar socializing.* A wolf-friendly environment is one where there is a *reason* for the Social Wolf's presence (*watching sports if they're sports fans, hanging out with friends they know well, etc*). A wolf will almost always prefer an environment he/she knows well.

Social Wolves enjoy familiar social environments that:

1.  **Allow for predictable social interactions in a public area.** Wolves like to know what to expect, especially at public outings. This is not to say that Wolves do not handle unpredictable social interactions well, as many of them do; rather, Wolves like to know generally what to expect in a social situation, especially if it involves people they don't know.

2.  **Enable them to discuss topics with others who share common interests.** Wolves love discussing topics that interest them, and often have friends who have similar hobbies and interests. They may enjoy people who are different from them, especially when these individuals have similar interests or have expertise in a subject that intrigues them.

3.  **Allow them to debate, express, or share their knowledge about an area of expertise.** Wolves almost always respect someone's expertise in an area they enjoy, and love to share their knowledge about a topic they know well. Discussing common hobbies and activities builds rapport with Wolves.

    *In short: Social Wolves love to hang out with those closest to them while discussing their interests in a very familiar social environment they have visited many times before.*

**Wolf-Unfriendly Environments:** *Meaningless interaction.* Social Wolves can be very patient if they understand their purpose or role in an environment, but they may not enjoy themselves if there are no "reasons" for socializing—or better stated by a Social Wolf: "*why am I here again*"?

Social Wolves become restless or impatient after an *extended period of time* if:

1. **There appears to be no purpose for a long, drawn-out social interaction.** Social Wolves like people, but are stingy with their "personal time". They don't see the purpose in investing in people they share little in common with, and do not prefer to socialize for the sake of it unless they have a valid reason to (*such as a friend or spouse asking them to socialize with someone*).

2. **People in the environment have very different social styles, beliefs, or values than the Wolf** (*for example, if the Wolf is very reserved, formal, and appropriate, and another party is extremely outgoing, crude, and inappropriate*). Wolves know what they like and know what they don't like, and are rarely overtly rude. Instead, they will be dispassionately engaged in conversation (*e. g., smile less and become less animated when someone asks a question, or offer short, half-hearted responses to questions*) once they're "ready to go".

3. **Several people exhibit ignorance regarding a topic about which the Wolf is highly knowledgeable.** Ignorance is difficult for the Social Wolf. When an uninformed friend makes an inaccurate comment about a topic the Wolf knows much about, a Wolf will usually diplomatically debate the person using facts and mock them if the person disagrees or cannot refute their argument using facts—and usually drop the issue shortly thereafter. If they don't know the person well, the Wolf talks to their friends about the ignorance exhibited by the person at the event after the "socializing" is over (*keeping in mind the Wolf didn't want to socialize with this uninformed person in the first place*).

   *In short: Social Wolves hate socializing with a bunch of strangers they have nothing in common with, for a long period of time, especially if the people don't know what the hell they're talking about.*

# Hybrid Wolves: Who the Wolf Has to Be

The Wolf prefers familiar socializing—and dislikes meaningless interaction.

But Wolves reside in various social settings, which limit the full expression of their activity drive.

That is, although Social Wolves prefer to focus on activities, they often choose to do other things, or their environments do not always allow them to focus on activities.

Environments do not always allow us to fully express our natural drives. When the Social Wolves are not able to express their activity drive, they will convert to a variation of the Social Wolf, or a Hybrid.

The first letter of each type (which is underlined) is the natural conflict style, whereas the remainder of the word is its hybrid adaptation—how the Wolf acts when expressing secondary drives.

Notice these Hybrids don't quite sound "right". Imagine a Kangaroo with a Wolf head, for example. This is who the Wolf can be, not who he/she is.

# Social Wolf: Hybrid Types

*Wangaroo:* This is the Social Wolf expressing her process drive. When Wolves are not concerned with what they're doing and are fully immersed in the moment, they will become the Wangaroo. The Wangaroo entertains and is extremely friendly with those they know as well as with those they don't know well. *This is how Wolves may behave when they are extremely relaxed or euphoric.*

*Wynx:* This is the Social Wolf expressing his group drive. Once Wolves have met their social needs, they often ensure other's needs are also met. They may often meet others needs before their own, especially those who mean a lot to them. *This is who Wolves may become when they are in a foreign social environment, they are relaxed, or there is no activity on which the group can center its attention.*

_Wanda:_ This is the Wolf expressing her <u>peace drive</u>. Wolves usually want harmonious relations so they and others can focus on the group task, not necessarily peace for its own sake. *Social Wolves will want peace for its own sake (like the Panda) usually only for a short period of time and/or when they are exhausted.*

_Wadger:_ This is the Wolf expressing his <u>truth drive</u>. Wolves usually try to extract the truth, using objective criteria as much as possible, when they are engaging in an activity that means much to them. *Many Wolves will have little trouble converting to the Wadger, but when doing so will become less concerned with personal details and emotions and more concerned with "what happened", or "the facts".*

# Wolf as the Rook

*Wolf Social Style*

## *Wolf Lifestyle*

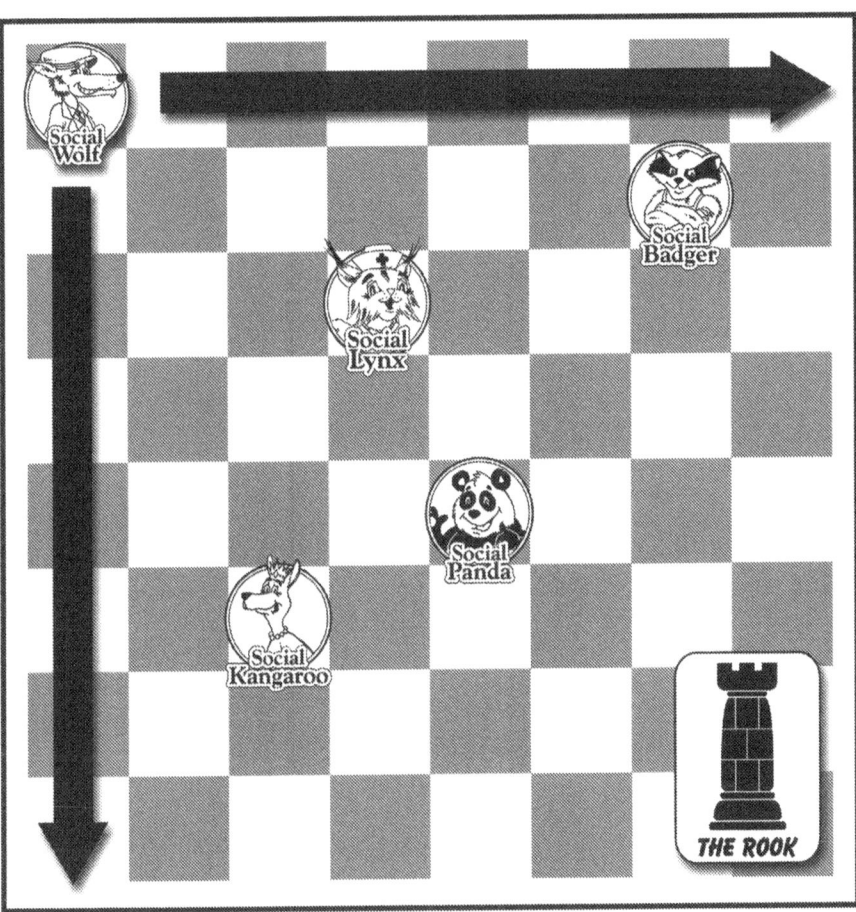

Similar to the Rook in Chess, the Social Wolf *prefers* to position in the corner of the board in order to:

- Stay in familiar social territory; i.e., spend time with friends with *similar interests.*

- Encourage people to play *on their territory* (the entire board) whenever possible—in this case, those close to them participate in an activity the Wolf and her/his social circle enjoy.

- By *specializing* in activities, the Wolf sets the tone for relationships with others they don't know very well.

# Social Lynx

## THE SOCIAL LYNX *(NOUN)*

*A SOCIAL CREATURE THAT PREFERS TO HELP OTHERS, USE TACT OR HUMOR TO DEFUSE CONFLICT, AND ENGAGE THE ENTIRE GROUP WHEN SOCIALIZING.*

*Conflict Style:* Lynx

*Social Drive: Group-driven:* the lifestyle of the Lynx is defined by connection to a group or a community.

*What draws a Social Lynx into conflict with other people?* When people's needs aren't being met in a group setting, Lynx's often use tact or humor to keep conflict from escalating. Because they dislike tension, Lynx's will attempt to keep conflict short and non-dramatic.

*When will a Social Lynx want to get out of conflict with another person?* Once they've addressed a group need and have "made a point", Lynx's tend to feel they've "won"—they are less concerned with "winning" and "losing" a conflict.

**Lynx-Friendly Environments:** *Collective environments.* A Lynx-friendly environment involves inclusion, adherence to social norms, and friendly interaction. Social Lynx's love the feeling of being in the presence of others, but usually prefer to disclose personal information only with those they know well.

Social Lynx's enjoy collective social environments that:

1. **Let them connect with others.** Lynx's usually share, and want others to feel comfortable in their presence. Often helpers or advice-givers, Social Lynx's like to focus on the other individual and feel they had a "meaningful conversation".

2. **Allow them to collaboratively acquire social status, especially around those they care about or admire.** Social Lynx's are sensitive to their status in a group, but don't want to offend others. Rather than attempting to dominate group members, Social Lynx's are more concerned with their niche in a group; that is, how they can contribute to a group and whether an individual obstructs their ability to influence the group in a positive way.

3. **Involve a mix of casual and formal interaction.** Lynx's enjoy socializing with others, and will attend both to group and individual needs. Unlike some other types, their behavior may differ slightly depending on whether they're interacting in a formal or casual environment; this skill makes them outstanding hosts or hostesses of social events.

**Lynx-Unfriendly Environments:** *Inconsiderate or indifferent environments.* A Social Lynx can be very patient if he/she can help others or sees progress in a not-so-friendly environment.

Social Lynx's become restless or impatient after an *extended period of time* if:

1. **People, or groups of people, are oblivious to the needs of others.** Social cultures that are inconsiderate of people in general or invalidate the needs of the Lynx will not be received well by the Lynx. The

Lynx will usually be polite—but these polite gestures will often be exaggerated or forced to conceal the Lynx's true feelings.

2. **People are too crude or inappropriate.** Social Lynx's love jokes and will kid around but usually don't prefer to be inappropriate in some settings, if doing so makes other people uncomfortable. The exception to this rule is if people are being too uptight and the Lynx decides to lighten up the group or someone "breaks the ice" with a racy joke or gesture that is well received by the group—this gives the Lynx "permission" to let their hair down and let loose.

3. **An individual must always have their way at the expense of others or someone refuses to adhere to social norms.** A Lynx might expect people to understand social rules or norms, or might attempt to incorporate an individual with poor social skills into their group—if someone rejects the Lynx's (genuine) invitation to join the group and continues to cause problems for him/her and others, the Lynx often interprets this as a personal slight.

# Social Lynx: Hybrid Types

- *Langaroo:* This is the Social Lynx expressing his <u>process drive</u>. When Lynx's are not concerned with group needs, they will often entertain. They will focus more on having fun and may tease lightheartedly—but usually not for too long. *This is how Lynx's often behave when they are relaxed, not focusing on a specific goal, or trying to get someone's attention.*

- *Lolf:* This is the Social Lynx expressing her <u>activity drive</u>. Lynx's balance activities with people—and will sometimes become immersed in an activity or doggedly pursue a goal—thus resembling the Social Wolf. *This is what Lynx's often become when they become competitive or focused on attaining a goal.*

- *Landa:* This is the Social Lynx expressing his <u>peace drive</u>. Lynx's usually want harmonious relations so they and others can focus on the group task, not peace for its own sake. *Social Lynx's will convert to the Landa when they want peace for its own sake (like the Panda) , usually for a short period of time, when they are exhausted.*

- *Ladger:* This is the Social Lynx expressing her <u>truth drive</u>. Lynx's will try to extract the truth using objective criteria when they are engaging in an activity that means much to them. *Social Lynx's are likely to convert to the Ladger when they are extremely frustrated or irritated.*

# Lynx as the Bishop

*Lynx Social Style*

## *Lynx Lifestyle*

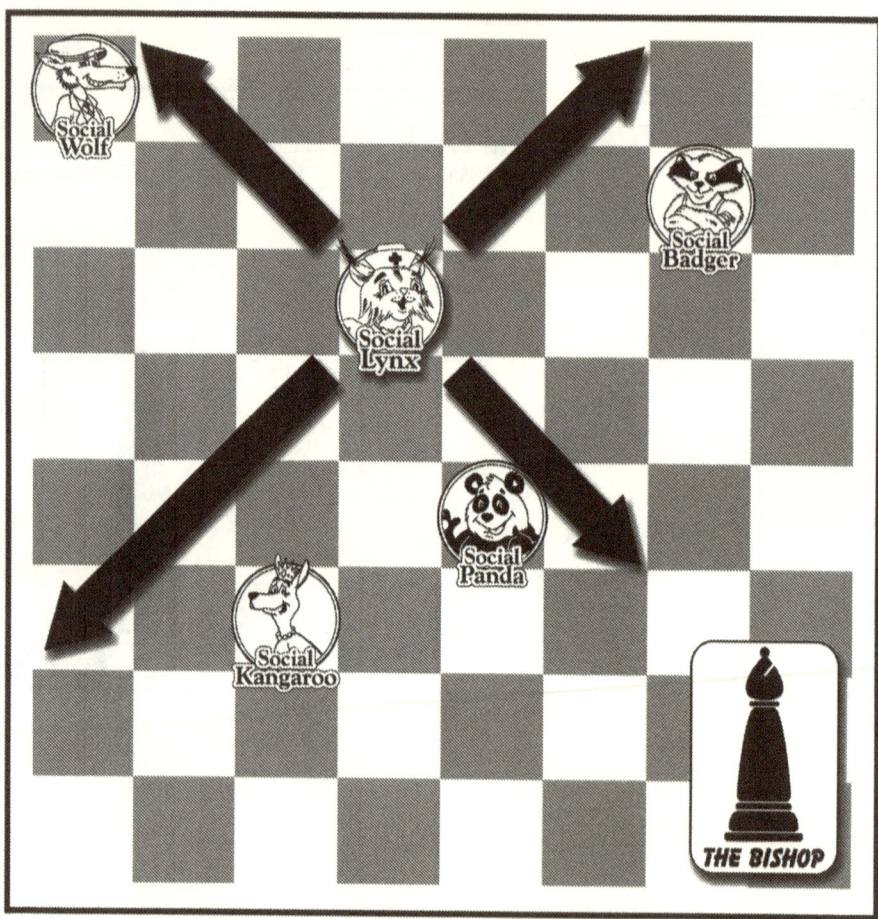

Similar to the Bishop in Chess, the Social Lynx *prefers* to position in the center of the board in order to:

- *"Host"* the group by helping other group members—this could come in the form of giving advice or listening—or even telling people what to do.

- Find their "niche" by discovering people's *needs* in the group and acting to address these needs.

- Better access *information* within the group, which assists in the expression of their group drive.

# Social Panda

## THE SOCIAL PANDA *(NOUN)*

*A SOCIAL CREATURE THAT PREFERS TO BE FLEXIBLE, RANDOMLY SOCIALIZE IN GROUPS OR ONE-ON-ONE TO MAINTAIN HARMONY, AND IS LESS CONCERNED WITH "WINNING" AND "LOSING" CONFLICTS.*

*Conflict Style:* Panda

*Social Drive: Peace-driven*: the lifestyle of the Panda is defined by stability and harmonious relationships.

*What draws a Social Panda info conflict with other people?* Because the Panda is quite flexible, someone usually must cross the line for the Panda to engage in conflict. Once the Panda "loses it", which is rare, it is memorable to those close to them—because conflict goes against their true nature.

*When will a Social Panda want to get out of conflict with another person?* As soon as possible and immediately if they've calmed down. They rarely see conflict in terms of "winners" and "losers". To a Panda, going to battle with someone else (perhaps even a very heated debate) is a loss.

**Panda-Friendly Environments:** *Collaborative environments.* Panda-friendly environments are harmonious, flexible, and diverse, allowing people to be themselves with little potential for conflict. The Panda is the most diverse type—some Social Pandas are laid back, some are hyper, and some are a mixture of both calm and hyperactive temperaments. All Pandas share one characteristic, however—they strive to get along with others.

Social Pandas enjoy collaborative social environments that:

1. **Are relaxing and peaceful.** Pandas like to escape from it all (*i.e., everyday stresses*). Because they often "go with the flow", the Social Panda often gets distracted from a goal in order to accommodate the needs of others. If a Panda becomes overly flexible, their environment becomes too hectic, and they need to escape to "reset".

2. **Allow them to do various things to stay occupied, but progress at their own pace.** Pandas are most effective when they have control over their environment but can also converse with others. Desiring harmony above all else, Social Pandas want to relax and enjoy life and the company of others important to them, but they often have trouble pleasing everyone, especially the most demanding people in their lives.

3. **Are harmonious.** Pandas can get along with most people for a while. They're quite flexible—and prefer that people are getting along.

**Panda-Unfriendly Environments:** *Hostile environments.* A Social Panda can be very patient if people aren't getting along, and may even mediate. But …

Social Pandas become restless or impatient after an *extended period of time* if:

1. **Someone they know well is inconsiderate or rude.** If someone close to the Panda apologizes quickly, they are likely to forgive and forget—however, blatantly disregarding the Panda's input, will, over time, cause the Panda to resent the other person. Pandas may then communicate their dissatisfaction with the relationship overtly—but they are much more likely to communicate their dissatisfaction

covertly or discuss their dissatisfaction with someone else other than the individual they're upset with.

2.  **Their considerate nature is unappreciated, or worse—they are punished for being considerate.** Few things upset Pandas more than not being appreciated for being considerate of others, or being sensitive to someone else's needs—especially if there was a lot of suffering involved.

3.  **Everyone is arguing and things are going nowhere.** Pandas have little tolerance for tense or conflicting situations, and even less tolerance for arguing for no reason. They will let something go just to end a conflict, or remove themselves from the situation altogether. Passive-aggressive behavior and unnecessary conflict also stresses out Social Pandas.

# Social Panda Hybrid Types

- *Pangaroo:* This is the Social Panda expressing his <u>process drive</u>. Pandas will entertain when they are in familiar social territory. For example, when they are around people they know well, they might convert to the Pangaroo and entertain. *This is how Pandas often behave when they are relaxed and feel free to express their true selves.*

- *Polf:* This is the Social Panda expressing her <u>activity drive</u>. A Panda is usually not interested in doggedly pursuing a goal, especially if the goal comes at the expense of important people in their lives. *This is how Pandas often behave if they have asked for input about a decision and have received no feedback about how to proceed from people they care about.*

- *Pynx:* This is the Social Panda expressing his <u>group drive</u>. Pandas more easily convert to the Pynx, modifying their behavior from an individual to a group-centered orientation. *Pandas convert to the Pynx when they feel the group isn't being taken care of or they are unsure about how to behave.*

- *Padger:* This is the Social Panda expressing her <u>truth drive</u>. Pandas will convert to the Padger only when necessary, and this expression is usually triggered by anger. Pandas, less concerned about who is right and wrong and more concerned about people, will reluctantly pursue the "truth" relentlessly as the Padger. *Pandas will convert to the Padger when they have had enough and given people many chances to get along with them.*

# Panda as the Queen

*Panda Social Style*

**THE SOCIAL PANDA**
THE PANDA POSITIONS TO PRESERVE HARMONY ON THE
BOARD BY RANDOMLY (GROUP & ONE-ON-ONE SOCIALIZING)
INTERACTING WITH FRIENDS.

THE SOCIAL PANDA MOVES
LIKE THE QUEEN IN CHESS.

THE QUEEN

*Panda Lifestyle*

Similar to the Queen in Chess, the Social Panda *prefers* to position in the center of the board in order to:

- Determine, in the moment, how to best maintain the *stability* of the group by preserving harmony.

- Allow the other pieces on the board to be *themselves*.

- Be *flexible* and avoid/prevent conflict—this is their true nature.

# Social Kangaroo

**THE SOCIAL KANGAROO** *(NOUN)*

*A SOCIAL CREATURE THAT PREFERS TO ENTERTAIN FRIENDS IN RANDOM WAYS BY KEEPING THINGS "INTERESTING", LIKES TO WIN QUICKLY, AND IS MORE GROUP THAN INDIVIDUALLY FOCUSED WHEN SOCIALIZING.*

*Conflict Style:* Kangaroo

*Social Drive: Process-driven*: the lifestyle of the Kangaroo is defined by entertaining others and/or process—process means "less concern with the goal than living in the moment". This is a playful style—but not everyone is a Kangaroo (but everyone is Kangaroo-like at times!).

*What draws a Social Kangaroo into conflict with other people?* In an attempt to keep things "interesting", Kangaroos often "stir things up". On the other hand, Kangaroos become uncomfortable with too much conflict—and prefer things simply stay "interesting" (but not too chaotic).

*When will a Social Kangaroo want to get out of conflict with another person?* If they're bored, tired of fighting, or the conflict has gotten out of hand, the Kangaroo will want out. The Kangaroo likes to "win" quickly.

<u>Kangaroo-Friendly Environments</u>: *Informal, fun environments.* Kangaroo-friendly environments are lively, not serious, and spontaneous.

Social Kangaroos enjoy informal, fun social environments that:

1.  **Involve a lot of joking and possibly sarcasm.** Kangaroos love people, and enjoy discussing irony. They rarely choose to become serious unless they are adapting to the expectations of others or they're in a formal situation. Social Kangaroos love dirty jokes and innuendos.

2.  **Allow them to be the center of attention.** Kangaroos love attention. They often entertain their friends and sometimes take a joke too far—or seem oblivious to what a group is doing because they're acting out for fun.

3.  **Enable them to socialize for the sake of it.** Although Kangaroos love relationships, they enjoy going into "social mode", where the goal is only to socialize and have fun—and little else. They often allow unexpressed aspects of themselves to surface, and may do certain things for shock value.

<u>Kangaroo-Unfriendly Environments</u>: *Stuffy, serious environments.* A Social Kangaroo can be very patient in a serious environment. But …

Social Kangaroos become restless or impatient after an *extended period of time* if:

1.  **Things become too routine or predictable. Kangaroos love to keep things "interesting".** Kangaroos usually dislike schedules and routine, unless a close friend needs something that requires them to do something routine or predictable. When restless, a Kangaroo might spend less time socializing with others and have less energy—leading them to want to "get out" and express themselves, usually in public.

2.  **People insist on social "rules" being followed.** Kangaroos don't follow social rules unless someone they respect feels strongly about rules—and has a good reason to. Kangaroos may cross the line before

they know they have taken things too far. It is important to Kangaroos that that things they do for shock value aren't taken too seriously.

3.  **Someone close to them is insulted by someone the Kangaroo doesn't know, respect, or like.** Kangaroos defend those they care about, and are less concerned about being popular or embracing the entire group (*unlike the Lynx for example*). They will fiercely defend people they care most about, but their anger rarely lasts for long. Irritation and anger usually comes and passes with Kangaroos, and then they're on to their next adventure.

# Social Kangaroo: Hybrid Types

- *Kynx:* This is the Social Kangaroo expressing his group drive. As the Kynx, Kangaroos will engage the entire group rather than those they know best. *This is how Kangaroos often behave when they are very relaxed, have been in the company of familiar and unfamiliar company for a prolonged period of time, or they just feel like it.*

- *Kolf:* This is the Social Kangaroo expressing her activity drive. Kangaroos pursue goals in a different manner than the Wolf, but resemble the activity-driven nature of the Wolf as the Kolf. Rather than pursuing a goal in a step-by-step fashion, the Kolf will just jump in—with motivation fluctuating throughout the process. *This is what Kangaroos become if they have not achieved a goal on time or are far behind schedule.*

- *Kanda:* This is the Social Kangaroo expressing his peace drive. Kangaroos like to get along with others, but not at any cost—unless they have to make nice for a formal occasion or for a close friend. *Social Kangaroos become the Kanda if they have no other option, if they're tired, or if they don't know the person well and don't care.*

- *Kadger:* This is the Social Kangaroo expressing her truth drive. The Kangaroo will extract the "truth", relentlessly if necessary, but usually only if necessary. Kangaroos don't take long to get over arguments and disagreements, but will corner someone if they are insulted for no reason. *Social Kangaroos will become the Kadger if they are upset by someone they care a lot about.*

# Kangaroo as the Knight

*Kangaroo Social Style*

## Kangaroo Lifestyle

Similar to the Knight in Chess, the Social Kangaroo *prefers* to position in one of the quadrants of the board in order to:

- *Live in the moment*, i.e., not focus solely on the group activity or goal.

- Socialize *sporadically*—with whoever wants to have fun.

- *Entertain* his/her friends—sometimes at their own expense (teasing, but not taken too far).

# *Social Badger*

## THE SOCIAL BADGER *(NOUN)*

*A SOCIAL CREATURE THAT PREFERS TO ADVOCATE OR PROTECT, KNOWS WHO HE/SHE LIKES AND DOESN'T LIKE, AND MUST BE RESPECTED BY AN ADVERSARY BEFORE ENDING A CONFLICT.*

*Conflict Style:* Badger

*Social Drive: Truth-driven:* The lifestyle of the Badger is defined by worthy causes—protecting people they care most about or advancing a worthy "mission" (their "truth"). They respect those that respect them.

*What draws a Social Badger info conflict with other people?* The Badger doesn't mean to conflict with others—it just happens—*who the Badger is* draws the Badger into conflict with others, and advocating a cause brings them into conflict as well.

*When will a Social Badger want to get out of conflict with another person?* Only once they've gotten the other person's respect. Don't piss the Badger off, ok?

<u>Badger-Friendly Environments:</u> *Respectful environments.* Badger-friendly environments allow Badgers to be themselves, protect those they care about, and relax.

Social Badgers enjoy casual environments that:

1.  **Allow them to "let their hair down".** Badgers hate compromising who they are. And it doesn't take much to make them feel this way—they like to be genuine and authentic, so being in an environment where they can say whatever's on their mind without having to worry about politics is a great environment for a Badger.

2.  **Talk about people that they admire and despise.** Badgers know who they like and who they don't like. And they enjoy venting about people they don't like. It's fun for them to "talk trash" about people that frustrate them. This venting process makes them less likely to take their frustration out on the person they despise if they can talk about "what they'd like to do".

3.  **Let them advise someone about a problem they've had in the past.** Because Badgers have often had to overcome a problem by willpower, they enjoy mentoring someone who is going through a similar situation. They might even do the person a favor to lighten their load.

<u>Badger-Unfriendly Environments:</u> *Formal environments.* A Social Badger can be very patient in a formal environment. But …

Social Badgers become restless or impatient after an *extended period of time* if:

1.  **Someone they care about is upset.** Badgers are very protective of people they're close to. It is very difficult for Badgers to "bite their tongues" if someone has harmed a close friend, but Badgers can show restraint—assuming they let the person who has wronged their friend know what they've done or vent to someone—a lot.

2.  **They're asked to be someone they're not.** Badgers must be real. Authenticity is critical for Badgers, so being themselves is very important—lest they become angry or shut down altogether.

3.  **An enemy makes a sarcastic comment about someone or something the Badger feels passionate about.** The Badger takes issues person-

ally, even when something doesn't necessarily have anything to do with them. Someone in the present often reminds them of someone they had issues with in the past, and they often conflict with these people—they sometimes just "fall into conflict".

# Social Badger: Hybrid Types

- *Bangaroo:* This is the Social Badger expressing her <u>process drive</u>. Badgers love good company, and will be themselves, often at great cost. Once relaxed and in familiar company, they may entertain. *A Badger will become the Bangaroo if they are relaxed and others have shown them respect.*

- *Bolf:* This is the Social Badger expressing his <u>activity drive</u>. Badgers achieve goals on their own terms rather than worrying about the expectations of others. Converting to the Bolf comes easily for Badgers, who will set aside feelings to achieve a common goal if they respect the mission and the crew. *Social Badgers become Bolves if they want to achieve a specific goal and have the means to do so.*

- *Banda:* This is the Social Badger expressing her <u>peace drive</u>. Badgers will not convert to the Banda without serious consideration or unless they have respect for someone. *Social Badgers will convert to the Banda only if they respect their adversary and can justify why.*

- *Bynx:* This is the Social Badger expressing his <u>group drive</u>. A Badger will respect others they have less in common with once they are relaxed or are feeling good about themselves. *Social Badgers will convert to the Bynx only if they know the people well or are extremely relaxed.*

# Badger as the King

*Badger Social Style*

## Badger Lifestyle

Similar to the King in Chess, the Social Badger *prefers* to position in one of the quadrants of the board in order to:

- Spend time with people they care most about—Badgers are very *loyal* to close friends.

- *Advocate* on someone's behalf—they stand up for those who advance their causes.

- *Cautiously* invest in other people—they have been burned before.

# Distinguishing Types

What differentiates one piece on the board from another? Glad you asked. In group settings with others they know well, the following guidelines help differentiate the pieces.

- Social Wolves and Social Badgers are similar in that they both tend to be one-on-one conversationalists. You can tell if someone is a Wolf or a Badger because their attention is usually *consistently* directed at specific individuals rather than at the entire group. Wolves and Badgers are different because Badgers usually take conflict more personally than Wolves. Wolves don't "conflict" as much as they disagree about something specific. Badgers conflict—and sometimes fight or feud—often with the same people—over and over again, whereas Wolves are more socially directed toward activities and rarely invest in enemies—they just attempt to outperform or outshine adversaries in a certain activity.

- Social Lynx's and Social Kangaroos are similar in that they both tend to be group conversationalists. Both types enjoy talking to others for fun—and usually attend to the entire group (or several group members) when conversing. Kangaroos are more likely to pay considerably more attention to certain group members than others, whereas Lynx's traditionally attempt to engage the entire group. The biggest difference between Kangaroos and Lynx's is their conflict style—Kangaroos enjoy "light drama", such as teasing, ragging, and racy jokes, whereas Lynx's are usually more formal and considerate—and avoid conflict unless cornered or angry.

- Social Wolves and Social Kangaroos are quite different. Wolves are one-on-one conversationalists, and Kangaroos are group conversationalists. Wolves will engage in conflict to WIN, whereas a Kangaroo usually conflicts with others for FUN. Kangaroos back off if they're not angry, whereas Wolves will fight to win a conflict for their egos' sake. A Wolf and Kangaroo may behave similarly when they're both having fun, though!

- Social Lynx's and Social Badgers are different in some ways. Lynx's are group conversationalists, whereas Badgers are one-on-one conversationalists. Lynx's and Badgers both take conflict personally, but Badgers don't let people get away with things they way Lynx's do—if offended, a Badger will give someone a glare—at the very least. And if upset, a Badger fights or chews someone out, whereas a Lynx usually tries to understand or resolve the issue if possible.

- Social Lynx's and Social Wolves are different in some ways. Lynx's are group conversationalists, and Wolves are one-on-one conversationalists. Wolves take conflict less personally than Lynx's; the Wolf strives to win rather than get personally involved—the Wolf's issue is usually a "topic" or "activity".

- Social Badgers and Social Kangaroos are different in some respects. Kangaroos are group conversationalists, whereas Badgers are one-on-one conversationalists. Badgers take conflict more personally than Kangaroos, and are more attached to conflict outcomes as well. Badgers, when angered, want to win and get respect, whereas Kangaroos want to engage and have fun. Kangaroos will back off and disengage if bored—Badgers rarely, if ever, back off in this manner.

- Social Pandas are different from other types, because they are random conversationalists. I realize that by putting them in their own unique category, many people may want to be "unique" and identify with the Panda. The Panda retreats from conflict altogether, unless threatened, and is quite unlike the other four types.

# The Seven "Laws" of Group Dynamics

Now that we've reviewed the pieces (or social animals) on the Social Chessboard, the "laws" governing these pieces will be reviewed. These laws are so reliable that you can bet they will, to some extent, be present in every situation.

Some of these laws are quite simple, others more complicated. All can be easily forgotten in the moment—at your peril.

Whether you're interacting with people you know well or complete strangers, keep these seven laws in mind to better understand how people interact in various situations.

*The Social Chess Board—The Seven Laws of Group Dynamics*

Here they are! The seven "laws" of group dynamics!

What should you do once you know these laws? Will you be able to take over the world? Master all of your personal relationships?

No—but know these laws when you see them—because they are everywhere and they govern all human interactions in group situations!

# THE SEVEN LAWS OF GROUP DYNAMICS

Law #1: Some people have collective conversational styles, whereas others have one-on-one conversational styles.

Law #2: The social fabric of groups is always uneven, but this unevenness is more visible in smaller groups.

Law #3: The social cultures of some groups lean far to the "social right"—a rigid hierarchy often forms in these groups.

Law #4: The social cultures of some groups lean far to the "social left"—these groups often resist strong direction.

Law #5: Tightening group fabric too quickly undermines relationships within a group.

Law #6: Sometimes the role overpowers the person, and sometimes the person overpowers the role.

Law #7: Social cultures fall between status quo and malleable.

# Law #1: Some people have collective (group) conversational styles, whereas others have one-on-one conversational styles.

Some people, such as the author of this book, prefer to talk to everyone in a group. This is true even if I don't know anyone in a group and I'm just stopping by.

Talking to everyone in a group has its advantages.

Take the example of Brian.

> *Brian ran into his coworker, Carly, at the mall. Carly was talking to a guy she had just met. After saying hello to Carly and talking with her briefly about work, Brian said goodbye and said he would see her later in the week.*

What went wrong here?

Brian didn't do anything "wrong". This is a normal social interaction that happens every day in the United States.

What Brian didn't know was that Carly was slightly embarrassed by his stopping by.

What Brian failed to notice was that Carly had just met a guy (Jim) she *liked* in the mall—for the first time. Jim was a friend of her friend Rachel. Carly had seen Jim at a cookout a week earlier, but they had not been introduced—and they were having their first conversation in the mall.

Brian was just saying hello—as he should have.

Brian was simply being polite.

Carly was thinking, "I kind of like Jim, and we're having a great conversation.

This guy can talk! And now he probably thinks I like this guy Brian!"

Guys—women do think this way sometimes.

Brian could have taken the time to introduce himself to Jim, and say, "Hey—I'm

Brian, I work with Carly—how's it going?".

Collective conversationalists *acknowledge* the entire group if possible—especially if the group is small, such as 3 to 5 people. Everyone in the group will appreciate being acknowledged, and you easily figure out how well everyone in the group knows each other.

Brian was Carly's coworker. Carly had just met Jim. Jim and Brian were strangers. Therefore, Carly was the one caught in the middle—she was the one who knew both of the other individuals in this group.

Brian, who approached Carly and Jim as they were immersed in conversation, could have introduced himself to Jim to make things easier on Carly—and Jim.

Brian didn't have to do anything—but Carly would have especially appreciated it.

Brian might have been in a hurry, and didn't have time to speak to the entire group. This is ok, in which case acknowledging Jim by nodding or smiling as he spoke would have been appreciated by Carly since Brian and Jim had not been introduced.

Carly could have introduced Jim and Brian, of course—but the onus is on Brian for interrupting their conversation.

Brian, however, is not a collective conversationalist—that is, he rarely engages the entire group when he talks.

This is not his style, and assessing the relationship between Carly and Jim was not his style.

When you're in a group, which do you prefer to do? Collective (group) or one-on-one conversation?

There are times to do both, but people are usually accustomed to one style more than the other.

Be able to do both, know which comes more naturally to you, and be aware of others' preferences as well.

# Law #2: The social fabric of groups is always uneven, but this unevenness is more visible in smaller groups.

The interweaving of relationships is what I call social fabric.

In any group, some people know one another better than others.

This is true regardless of how long a group has been together—25 years, 2 years, 6 months, or 15 minutes—or what its stated purpose is.

Think for a moment about your closest relationships. Some of your friends and family know things about you that others don't. You know you can reveal certain things to some people and not to others.

Guess what? This is true for other people as well.

Within any group, some people are closer to some group members than others. The social fabric of any group is unevenly woven together at any point in time, meaning some people are closer to some while more distant to others. Social fabric resets itself often in the early stages of group formation, until interactions evolve into relationships—resulting in the natural occupation of niches within different social circles.

One person may have a reputation for being "difficult" in one circle of friends, while being gentle and less direct in another.

Such is the nature of group interaction, especially once relationships have been formed.
In groups that have been together for long periods of time, the social fabric is often very uneven.

Take the following example:

*David, Jerry, Kevin, and Ron worked together on a sales team for 4 years at a large bank. For the first 6 months they worked together, the four of them were inseparable at work and often went to lunch and played golf together on weekends. As time progressed, the relationships between the four of them changed—David and Ron became closer friends, while Jerry and Kevin made friends with people outside the sales department and spent less time with David and Ron. Interestingly, the fact that Jerry and Kevin weren't spending as much time with David and Ron in extracurricular activities resulted in David and Ron becoming **closer friends**. Some animosity developed between the four of them; Jerry and Kevin talked about the tight friendship that David and Ron shared, claiming that they often showed favoritism by assigning each other lighter workloads whenever possible—Jerry and Kevin, although not personally close, confided in each other because they believed Ron and David were so close they were being excluded from some business decisions.*

Although this is a classic office politics example, it illustrates that social fabric is uneven in groups. Uneven social fabric will be especially visible in small groups when the groups have been formed for a specific purpose (such as work) and the people are together for a long period of time (such as a month or more).

People might be closer to one friend, but not as close to another—this phenomenon is true in any group. Also true is that someone might be very close to two people, but the nature of the persons' relationships is very different.

Cliques will form. People will embrace others while shunning other people. Such is the nature of groups.

# Law #3: The social cultures of some groups lean far to the "social right"—a rigid hierarchy often forms in these groups.

There is a "social right" and a "social left".

The social right and social left are not political philosophies, although politics do influence the actions of groups who adopt these mindsets.

More on the "social left" later.

Healthy groups on the "social right" have a flexible hierarchy and are formed for the purpose of an activity or business. Openly acknowledging differences in ability or status, promoting reasonable competition, and allowing people to express personal differences without subjection to ridicule are staples of the moderate social right.

Groups that fall extremely far to the "social right" have a rigid hierarchy that is enforced, have goals that center around an individual's personal interests, and are always suspect of outside influences.

"Far right social groups" are extremely homogenous; they consist of like-minded people, and anyone who dares to stand out, even in a constructive or helpful way, is deemed ignorant by its leadership. A mindset permeates this group, and a hierarchy forms—with only a few individuals at the top.

It is very clear who runs the show in these groups.

If a "far right social group" is small (and it usually is), then it is usually formed to achieve a specific objective—to advance the goals of its leader.

This can be a very strong-minded group, especially if it does not exist within the structure of a formal organization.

By the way, if you're working for an organization that has adopted this mindset, do yourself a favor and find another job.

If you're involved in a religion or social circle with this mindset, get a life—and help if necessary—and get out.

# Law #4: The social cultures of some groups lean far to the "social left"—these groups often resist strong direction.

Just as an extreme "social right" exists, the extreme "social left" exists as well—and serves to preserve a group at any cost. Extreme social left groups will not *publicly* acknowledge that individual interests can take precedence over collective interests, but this is often the case.

When groups are extremely socially (not ethnically) diverse, every individual holds a different view, and subgroups become unyielding in that view. The result is a more collective mindset—to preserve the collective (group) status quo.

Often a few individuals dominate the far left social group, but do so without the explicit acknowledgement of the group members.

When a group makes explicit claims to be equal, it uses delicate language to subvert evidence of inequality within it, creating a utopian standard of group harmony that people are not allowed to publicly challenge. Reframing language to protect subgroups and maintain the group is not evil—but it serves to preserve the group "status quo" at any cost.

An organization that has adopted this mindset will be constantly distracted by personal agendas, and individuals will rarely agree on the organization's mission.

Get another job if the organization is obsessed with discovering its group identity, because it will be threatened by strong direction from anywhere within its borders.
The answer to the group's problem will always lie elsewhere.

And attempts by individuals to take strong action will be met with firm resistance from the group.

Healthy groups on the "moderate social left" take care to ensure that individual as well as group needs are met. By allowing ambition and individual differences to naturally manifest themselves, the group acknowledges reality—and enables people to become who they naturally want to become within the group.

# Law #5: Tightening group fabric too quickly undermines relationships within a group.

People need time to get to know each other. And some people will reveal things about themselves much sooner than others.

Forcing people to reveal things about themselves before they're ready to do so is an attempt to tighten the social fabric of a group at a faster rate than is natural—and this unnatural process often undermines the way relationships evolve within a group.

Relationships have to play out naturally, without interference.

> *Gary moved to a new area and reconnected with an old childhood friend, Peter. Peter had always liked Gary, but remembered that he had an annoying habit—he often revealed too much about himself. Despite suspecting that Gary hadn't changed since childhood, Peter decided to invite Gary, now a young adult, to meet him and his friends for dinner.*
>
> *Much to Peter's chagrin, Gary shared intimate details about his personal life within minutes of sitting down at dinner. After discussing his mental health history, his failed marriage, and the fight he is currently having with his mother, Peter's friends were extremely annoyed with Gary. Although Peter knows Gary is a good guy and means well, Peter's friends labeled Gary as some-*

*one with a "lot of baggage" who reveals too much too early. Gary's actions made the evening awkward—and limited the quality of the relationships Gary can have with this group.*

Peter didn't do anything wrong. He was trying to help out an old friend.

As Peter learned, however, mixing close social circles with more distant social circles is not always a good idea.

If Peter had invited Gary to lunch before deciding to invite him along with his closer friends, he could have saved himself some unnecessary grief.

The fabric of any group must tighten at a rate that is appropriate for that group. This can be difficult to predict—sometimes, you just have to put people together to see how they will get along.

But take calculated rather than unnecessary risks.

You know your friends.

And you know who they might like and who they might not like.

Limit their exposure to people you suspect they might not like—and then see how they deal with new people—or you could affect the quality of your closest relationships.

# Law #6: Sometimes the role overpowers the person, and sometimes the person overpowers the role.

Expectations directly affect people's behavior.

Sometimes people will act they way they do because it's the way they are, and in another situation they are fulfilling the social obligations of a role they must play.

For example, consider the job interviewer and the interviewee.

*Jim is a hiring manager at a small company, and is a warm, sensitive person. His experiences have taught him that in order to interview effectively, one must not reveal too much to the interviewee. During the first few months as hiring manager, Jim was warm and sensitive with interview candidates. He discovered quickly, however, that job candidates often called him several times after the interview to inquire about their performance, even if Jim asked them not to do so.*

*In order to interview more effectively, Jim adopted a more suitable interaction style with job candidates. Rather than attempting to be cold and aloof (the opposite of how he actually is), Jim maintained a detached, sensitive style dur-*

*ing interviews. The "new Jim" was sending a different message to job candidates—that the company cared about them but that the interview was a professional, rather than a personal, meeting.*

By adopting a more suitable role, Jim was eliminating a lot of the confusion for the job candidate and himself.

Always consider the role the other person must play in an interaction.

# Law #7: Social cultures fall between status quo and malleable.

In status quo social cultures, social circles are rarely updated. Some people prefer to keep the same circle of friends throughout their lives. These individuals prefer to be "settled", and are comfortable keeping things the way they are, and often adopt a status quo mindset with their social life.

In progressive social cultures, social circles update regularly. These people like to meet new people regularly, and as a result, rotate their social circles. They enjoy having a wide circle of friends, and are bored when not provided with opportunities to meet new people.

Status quo and progressive social cultures are different. Status quo social cultures involve a leisurely lifestyle—whereas progressive social cultures involve a more active social lifestyle.

Status quo social cultures are tight-knit and are not as open to new people. Progressive social cultures welcome new experiences and new people.

Moderate social cultures have their own culture and welcome others in a cautious manner. Observe this.

# The Laws and the Pieces—Restoring Order to Chaos

Social Chess restores order to the chaotic nature of relationships—which always take place in group settings—for at least two people must be present for a relationship to exist. The seven laws of group dynamics offer safe assumptions to make in groups but stop short of providing information that enables or encourages the reader to manipulate group dynamics or relationships. Each of the conflict styles mentioned earlier must conform to the seven laws of group dynamics. All of these types engage in conflict with others, and it is when in conflict with those they know best that reveals their true social drive—what motives them in their closest relationships. To enhance one's understanding of groups and relationships, one must first position the pieces on the board, what drives these pieces, and then account for the laws governing the board itself.

Social Chess provides an observational case study approach that can enhance our understanding of the roles we occupy in our close relationships. Natural roles, whatever their form, are an inevitable phenomenon of nature. And I strongly believe that relationships, far from an exact science, can be better understood if theories with both empirical and autobiographical foundations are used to account for their complexity.

# A Note to Academics

Writing a dissertation that examined the relationship between conflict and personality helped me appreciate the complexities of interpersonal conflict in different situations from a detached perspective. My dissertation advisors helped me design a study that investigated how people assign blame when engaged in conflict with another person. Some people, we posited, must believe that the outcomes of conflict are attributable to themselves and the other party, whereas others are likely to perceive conflict outcomes as less personal, and therefore attribute conflict outcomes to situational factors. One of the implications of this empirical study, which employed a quantitative methodology, was that people perceive conflict situations differently and that these differences originate within the individual. I was excited to share these discoveries with my peers and advisors, but was more interested in discussing the implications of what I had learned in professional and personal settings. Although it is clear that the implications of empirical conflict research for society are legion, each time I speak formally with audiences outside of my field (*which for me is 99 percent of the time*) I am reminded that academic information must often be reframed in order to be appropriate for non-academic presentation and consumption.

The greatest challenge for any applied social scientist wishing to present information to a general audience is addressing both scientific and practical concerns. Academics with backgrounds in quantitative methods are often concerned with advancing theory, whereas the public (*and many readers of this book*) are primarily interested in learning about themselves and those they care much about. Social Chess, initially designed to offer a quantitative-based model that could advance conflict theory in the emerging field of organization development, evolved into a personalized account that can assist individuals with identifying their own, as well as others', conflict styles within established relationships.

Social Chess features five distinct conflict "profiles", each with four hybrid variations. These profiles are best understood as *qualitative group constructs* because they identify and conceptualize natural, often conflicting social niches people occupy in their close relationships. The profiles reviewed in this book can be observed in small and large groups in most professional and personal settings. All who are interested in discovering their own conflict styles, or the conflict style of someone they know well, can easily apply the information in this book—*immediately*.

# References

Social Chess was not designed to extend academic theory; however, the following works were consulted prior to the genesis of this project:

Beverly, C., Camden-Anders, S., & O'Toole, S. (2003). *Individual differences in situational attribution and a model of interpersonal conflict.* Applied dissertation completed at Alliant International University-Fresno.

Eade, J. (1999). Chess for Dummies. New York. Hungry Minds Inc.

Kilmann, R.H., & Thomas, K.W. (1977). *Developing a forced-choice measure of conflict-handling behavior: The "MODE" instrument.* Educational and Psychological Measurement, 37, 309—325.

*Social Chess,*[TM] *and all concepts, ideas, theories, included in this book are protected under copyright law.*

# About the Author

Dr. Chris Beverly is an applied social scientist who conducts and supervises experiential dissertations and studies in the United States. An expert on hybrid research designs, he has served as an adjunct professor of organization development at Alliant International University, an adjunct instructor of psychology at Reedley College and Valencia Community College, and an instructor at St. Johns River Community College. He is currently a group dynamics consultant for individuals and organizations.

978-0-595-43004-8
0-595-43004-X